SNARING SQUIRRELS

(AND OTHER WILDERNESS LESSONS FROM THE SQUACK)

Author: Jamie L. Burleigh
Contributing Author: Creek Stewart
Copyeditor: Jacob Perry
Photography/Illustrations: Jamie Burleigh

Wholesale inquiries please visit http://www.dropstonepress.com
Purchase this Pocket Field Guide and others in this series at
http://www.creekstewart.com

Published by DROPSToNE PRESS
978-1-947281-23-3

DROPSToNE
PRESS
dropstonepress.com

IMPORTANT DISCLAIMER:

Nearly all types of improvised survival traps are considered illegal outside of an actual survival scenario. Please check your local hunting/trapping laws before practicing or using survival-style traps, including this one.

"I HAVE A LOVE-HATE RELATIONSHIP WITH SQUIRRELS."

-JAMIE BURLEIGH

INTRODUCTION

Squirrels. I love to watch them, hunt them, trap them, and eat them. Nowadays, folks don't fully appreciate what a squirrel can provide for them, especially in a survival situation.

My hate could simply be ill feelings for those who do not understand the squillationship I have with an animal I could never really hate. If given a chance to watch a squirrel's daily routine, one could compare it to a masterful symphony detailing outdoor life. Squirrels are magnificent (in the trees AND on the dinner plate)!

First, let's begin to understand the critter we'll be discussing in the following pages. A Squack, a Squill, the Chicaree, a Tree Rat, and the Douglas—all common and not-so-common names for the squirrel. These names could be great trivial pursuit fodder or potentially lifesaving terminology, if you're ever lost in Appalachia!

Pine Squirrel (this genus includes the American Red,
Douglas, and Mearns's Squirrel)

In the North, squirrels are simply referred to as "reds." That name reflects the distinct red/blond coloration of the small forest dweller, and it was in a northern forest where I learned so much about them.

Fox squirrel, distinguished by its orange to bronze hues
and large bushy tales.

Squirrels belong to the same family of rodents (Sciuridae) as chipmunks, marmots, and prairie dogs. For the purposes of this field guide, however, we'll be discussing the varieties that spend most of their time in the trees. In North America and Canada, those tend to be one of five types of squirrels: Pine Squirrels (including the American Red, Douglas, and Mearns's Squirrel), Fox Squirrels, Black Squirrels, Eastern Gray Squirrels, and Western Gray Squirrels. All these tree-dwelling squirrels have similar habits, so it's not important that you be able to distinguish between each one of them (for survival at least). And, of course, all squirrels are edible.

I have a saying: "Find a nut and eat for a day. Find a squirrel and eat for a lifetime." In this guide, my goal is to teach you how to hunt squirrel and eat for a lifetime, should it ever become necessary.

THE SQUIRREL

When it comes to survival, the squirrel has much to teach us. Before we get into how to snare them, let's first discuss what these creatures can teach us and how they can positively impact survivability. The squirrel is an excellent survival instructor, and when you find one, you'll know that resources are plenteous in that area. Also, you'll never find just one. Furthermore, if you've found one squirrel, then you have found most of your resources to survive in the wild!

Squirrels live their entire lives within a few hundred yards of the same shelter, water, food, and family. Squirrels pick locations that will support themselves and a litter for all four seasons of the year. Thus, to reiterate the importance of this—if you've found a squirrel, you have found an area that will more than likely provide many basic resources for your survival. Let's discuss each one.

Lessons from the Squirrel: SHELTER

A squirrel's home needs protection from predators and four seasons of weather. Immediately after a young squill leaves its mother, they look for a suitable new home. The nesting area must be able to sustain a breeding pair and a lifetime of young litters. Squills seldom move far from others squills.

A smart squirrel, like a smart human fending for survival,
finds a home that's protected from the elements.

When you see one squirrel, there is a good chance there are
more nearby. They are a social creature and will infringe
on other familial feeding grounds until they outgrow their
welcome. Squirrels can live in trees, dead-falls, underground
burrows, log piles, your attic, and even in the rusted tailpipe
of your '57 Buick. NEVER underestimate the attraction
between a squirrel and good resources.

In the Northeast, squirrels prefer large stands of hardwood
and conifers because they provide plenty of food *and* shelter.
Take note of where the squirrels are most active. This will be a
place safe from large predators and filled with the very things
you, as a person, need to survive. If we are to learn anything
from squirrels, it is how to best utilize these specific locations
and resources to the fullest.

Among other survival resources, these squirrely locations provide:

- Quick cover/shelter
- Weather barriers
- Comfortable bedding/insulation
- Accelerants to help create/maintain fire
- Dry firewood/tinder
- Green boughs to burn black for signaling
- Needles/bark/sap for tea and medicine
- Pine nuts/bark for food

Lessons from the Squirrel: WATER & FOOD

Squirrels gather 10x more food per day than they consume, and most of their daily routine consists of foraging for food and drinking plenty of water. Squirrels need an abundance of water for healthy digestion, to maintain their high metabolism, and to nurse their young. If you observe and track a squirrel for a few hours, I can almost guarantee it will lead you to a clean water source! This is one of the most important survival lessons I could ever share with you. *Learn to TRACK THE SQUACK!*

A squirrel will almost always lead you to water.

When observing squirrels, do so from a distance. If they think there is a predator in the shadows or another rival squill, they will go into an open area with an escape easement and create a *distraction*. Squirrels will round a spot like an old hound dog circling its bed, dig a hole, and PRETEND to bury a nut. All of this is an elaborate attempt to provoke and flush out the predator or nut thief. It is quite the spectacle to watch in person!

what you need. In a survival situation it's either you or them. Do not think of it as stealing their food. Rather, think of it as saving their life. After all, if you don't eat the food the squirrel has gathered, you'd probably eat them!

Where a squirrel feeds is safe from predators. It's also a place where they let their guard down to investigate alternative food sources and curiosities. It's the perfect place for a trap or snare. I'll be teaching you how to make the perfect squirrel snare very soon.

Lessons from the Squirrel:
WEATHER PREDICTION

Squirrels are a great indicator for past, present, and future weather fronts. They will eat from old food caches while new forage is ripening. Take note of these past storage locations. It could tell you that during the winter that location could be buried in deep snow or may be covered by high water levels in the spring. This is invaluable information when it comes to picking a shelter site.

If the tree rats are frantically scavenging, burying, and scurrying about during most of the daylight hours, be assured that a change in the weather is quickly approaching. They need to store at least as much food as they consume

storm fronts hit and work closer to their food caches and homes during this time.

If you observe summer and fall food storage high in trees or rock caches, it will be a very harsh or long winter. High food storage means easy access when there is deep snow or ice.

Bottom line: watching a squirrel's routine is greatly beneficial to the survivor. They will inform you of weather fronts, where food is, and sometimes where they live. Never underestimate a squirrel's ability to teach you the ways of the wilderness. They are the ultimate survival instructors!

Territory map for reference.

My obsession with the wilder things started like it does for many others. As a kid, I ran to the woods looking for "big" game to hunt with my spring-action BB gun. I cut my teeth on local tree rats. I knew about local flora and fauna before I knew how to ride a bicycle. It took but a shiny glint from my trusty weapon to strike fear in the hearts of any beast that passed within its range.

my guide—a Mushkegowuk Cree—and travel further north to "good" hunting land near James Bay. For him, it was a chance to revisit his childhood hunting grounds and family. For me, it was a great opportunity for an adventure. Our mission was to clear family trap-lines for that winter's season and bring a young moose back for the local reserve community. He needed a ride, and I wanted to learn. It was a good trade and I was eager to oblige.

When I picked up my Cree Guide, Jim, at a local Canadian restaurant, he was dressed like an old logger—steel toed work boots worn at the toes, blue jeans ripped at one knee showing white long johns below, red plaid shirt rolled up exposing the same white long john undershirt pushed up to his elbows, and topped with a new Ski-Do trucker hat. His gear consisted of an oversized burlap sack over one shoulder and a large ax on the other. His front pocket carried an open box of cigarettes and his rear pocket held a red handkerchief.

"I'm Jim, friend of Black Bear, and you must be Jamie!"

Without hesitation I quickly answered. "Yes, Yes I am. Glad to finally meet you. Let's gather the rest of your gear and head north. We have another 8 hours to Smooth Rock to pick up our canoe."

"I have all that I need," Jim said.

spoken on the long, arduous ride. However, it wasn't long before Jim told me we could stay at his family's cabin. He referred to this cabin as "Moose Camp" and said we would be dry under its roof and that it was just a short walk from the logging road. I figured that is why he chose to bring such little gear.

Many hours had passed, and I was exhausted when we arrived at our destination. I let Jim look over the gear I had brought for the trip. He would know what equipment I needed for the week. He grabbed a few items and placed the excess behind the seat with a blanket to cover it up.

"Time to go," he said, and we were off to Moose Camp.

I hid my keys under the truck bed and quietly said "good-bye," as I was not expecting to see it when we returned!

At that point, I had to question the food we were leaving behind. "Won't we need food, Jim?"

"Nope, don't need anything else," he said confidently.

I asked, "How long since you've been at Moose Camp, Jim?"

"'Bout 12 years ago...maybe 15," he replied. With that, we began our journey into the unknown.

stood an old, galvanized feeding bucket turned woodstove. This was to be home for the next week, and I absolutely fell in love with it.

Jim was legendary, and from that point forward I had no idea my "outdoor life" would be forever changed. My adventures that week could fill many books, but I felt a short backstory about how I learned to snare red squirrel was important.

The pallet "cabin" was impressive in its own way, and I appreciate Moose Camp a little more every time I think about it. The bush is demanding but extremely rewarding.

For reference, my small pack contained:

• An extra flannel shirt
• Wool socks
• Matches
• Tea, coffee, salt, and sugar
• Metal cup and spoon
• Pull of rope
• Granola bar
• #24g wire

I also stowed a 3-bladed pocketknife in my front pocket, handkerchief in my rear pocket, and I carried an ax in leather-gloved hands. Jim carried even less. His "pack"

keep it centered over his shoulders, so he wrapped a wide strip of brain leather in the middle to create a comfortable handle and simply carried it like a briefcase most of the day. When the pillow sack was not twisted in the middle, he used the leather strap to connect opposite corners of the bag to sling across his body. He stuffed socks tightly into the inside corners of the bag to keep the strap from slipping. Jim said this is where he kept his keys, money, and matches. It was a very smart idea to keep valuables in these tight corners. It was a slick rig for sure.

HOW TO TRACK, BAIT, AND SNARE SQUIRREL FOR SURVIVAL

When we left the cabin on our first morning, we walked in a big circle around camp at a fast pace. Jim purposely walked loudly and advised me to do the same. We needed to make our presence known to the "reds" we were going to set for.

Jim looked back at me and noticed my concern. "You want to eat, don't you?" he asked with a raised brow.

We had walked in large circles for good reason and Jim asked if I had noticed the barking cadence as we walked. He said the barking squirrels were alerting others that danger was approaching. The small reds were high in the trees, sounding to one another—not loudly but consistently. The barking was less prevalent as we walked further from that location. Reds sounded off less the further we got from them. They let us know exactly how far their "curiosity" range extended by doing this.

Here is an example of a "mess." This is simply another word
for a squirrel feeding spot. Notice the chewed acorn litter
on top of the stump.

that a water source was near, and it was a good place to set snares. A good combination of food and water was an excellent place to make a set.

The "mess" was a word Jim used to describe cuttings and shell debris from the pine nuts, acorns, and other various seeds in the red's diet. Basically a "mess" was another word for a feeding spot. These feed spots were perfect locations to clear and make a snare pole set.

CLEARING THE SET

A squirrel pole is just that—a pole supporting a few wire snares set to catch squirrels. It is used as a bridge or passageway and capitalizes on a squirrel's instinctual travel habit and patterns. This set requires a small clearing near abundant squirrel "signs." This clearing provides an open vantage point for the squirrels to eat and survey. The poles provide escape routes and an even higher vantage point to look out over a great distance for predators.

To begin setting a proper squirrel pole, make your clearing better than any other. Remove all other low vantage points—this could be large sticks, branches, or dead leaning trees in your immediate area. This is noisy work, but do not worry.

Remove dead leaning trees.

Example of other vantage points to take down when clearing
a site for a squirrel pole.

Do not worry about making noise when clearing your set. It will attract curiosity from nearby squirrels. Just like all alarms, they need to be investigated but at a SAFE DISTANCE. Use these commonalities and traits. This trait is why the squirrel pole snares work so well.

Curiosity killed MORE than just the cat! Squirrels are incredibly curious critters! Be quick—do your business and leave. It will give the squirrels a show and they will soon investigate why you re-arranged their living room!

I was directed by Jim to clear an area about 15 feet in diameter on the ground where we would set the squirrel poles. Jim removed all dead branches from about 7 feet high down to the ground using his ax. I cleared the ground by shuffling my feet.

Next, he gathered the poles. Jim chose long, living, and straight saplings to create "ridgepoles" for the set. The ridgepoles were no larger than my forearm at the largest end. This is to assure no "run-a-rounds." A run-a-round is when a squirrel goes all the way around the pole. It is much easier for them to do this on larger poles. When making a prime squirrel "roadway," be sure to only offer ONE LANE to travel. This was great advice!

When traveling this pole, there is only one way to go,
and that's right through the wire noose.

FORMING THE WIRE SNARES

Jim dropped his bag and retrieved a small metal cup. Nestled snugly inside was thin green utility wire, wound in circular fashion. He pulled out a few premade snares and showed me how simple they were to make right off the spool.

Jim bought the wire recommended for snaring squirrels at a large hardware chain store. The 24 gauge garden wire he favored came in a compact container that was green in color and came with a handy cutting tool attached. This is exactly what I'd suggest you keep in your survival trapping kit also (Order link if interested: https://amzn.to/3hYcchw).

The wire was cut at an average length of pull from the center of his chest to outstretched fingertip—my guess would be approximately 30 inches. He then wrapped one end of the wire loosely around the tip of his pinky finger and, with a few twists, he was done creating the noose-eyelet of the snare.

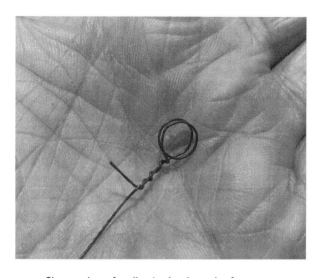

Close-up photo of small, twisted eyelet used to form noose.
Notice the bent wire tag pointed inward—the is a **KEY** detail.

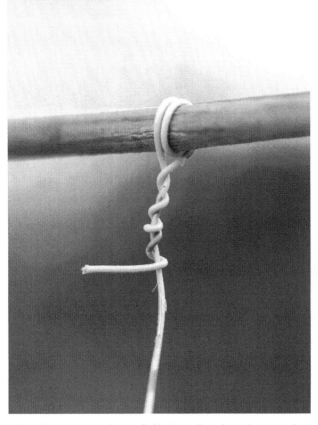

A small branch, about the size of a No. 2 pencil, can be used to create the eyelet. Notice the wire is wrapped twice around the branch.

place 3 or 4 of his fingers comfortably within the loop he created.

After the noose was complete, the small sharp tag end of the noose-eyelet was pointed inside the finished snare loop. This end of the wire dug into the squirrel's hide, further irritating the catch. This unique feature made the victim flail around more, further tightening the snare around its neck. This made for a quick, clean kill. The short tag end was just as important as the snare loop itself.

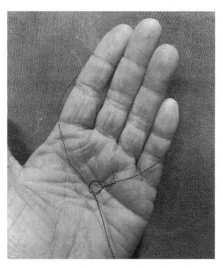

3–4 fingers in width is the ideal diameter of a squirrel pole wire snare.

of the snare loop should be about 2 inches from the top of the pole and stable from winds or foul weather.

Notice how the snare is secured to the pole and the excess wire is wrapped around the base to help support the snare in an upright position. Also note the 2-finger height of the snare above the pole.

SNARE LOCATION ALONG POLE

Snare location is very crucial when using a snare pole. You do not want to waste a good snare by setting it in a location where there is no traffic. Jim set a snare in the middle of the pole and a few feet apart on each side. That was it. He told me that squirrels like to jump and cut off sharp corners for speed and efficiency. I have yet to see a squirrel or any other jumping critter utilize a tight inside corner.

The reds like to utilize the inside corners for a perch and so they can feed safely with a view. After some time, they get used to the setup and are more comfortable using the ramp and horizontal pole for travel to their best new feeding location. This is when their guard is down. They are comfortable with the set. This is when you will catch the most. Jim's theory was sound.

Example of inside corner on horizontally positioned snare pole.
Notice the wire snare positioned about 2 feet from the corner.
The green wire is barely visible.

The approaching "ramp" is supported by the ridge pole and secured to the tree on one side. It had snares set, just 2 in the middle, splitting the 8-foot length.

Horizontal ridgeline snare pole with diagonal ramp snare pole.
The gloves in photo indicate wire snare locations for this set.

Flashy CD dangling from string in the middle of the
15-foot radius cleared area.

Now that the 'set' was live and ready with snares, Jim wanted to add a lure. A lure is an attractive curiosity to the animal. That day, it was a small piece of ribbon cut from his red kerchief. It was tied on a small stick and pushed into the ground about 10 feet away from the pole in the middle of the clearing. This was to pique the squirrel's interest. This distraction was something left behind that they would focus on, INSTEAD of the new snares that lay in their path to this new feeding site!

The squirrels would never approach from the ground and would use the squirrel pole for a better view! I witnessed this firsthand. This visual distraction should be something out of the ordinary. A piece of plastic or trash. A feather on a string. A soup can resting on a stick pushed into the ground. In our case it was a torn strip of Jim's red bandanna!

Plastic bottle trash lure.

If you want to eat, you set snares.

A wide angle picture of the perfect Squirrel Pole Set.

It was now 10am and we were still within view of camp. As we walked away, I was advised by Jim to make lots of noise, and break branches as we left the snare pole area just created. It felt counterintuitive to me, but I did as I was told.

resources. If they did leave, another family unit would quickly take over the vacancy.

He said that it was almost a "perfect set" and that he felt confident that we would eat red soup that evening. I was hopeful.

SQUIRREL SOUP
FOR DINNER

It got dark quickly under the dense canopy, and after a day's hard work doing other camp chores, it was finally time to check the snares! As we approached the set, aggressive barks and chatter greeted us. There was one squirrel hanging neatly by its neck in the middle snare on the snare pole and another using the inside corner as a perch feeding.

Red Squirrel hanging from Squirrel Pole

dinner from the squirrel pole.

"No re-sets tonight," Jim muttered.

"We will do the same thing tomorrow. Go fetch some water so we can eat."

He explained to me that the reds will not move for the rest of the evening. Predators would be out. The great horned and snow owl, along with lynx and many others would hunt the night. They would be there tomorrow, carrying on as usual. The only difference is that we would, too!

By the time I filled the large soup pot with water, Jim had shucked the hide clean from the tiny red squirrel and had entrails separated. The guts were saved to be placed on hooks in the stream. This provided us with the best brook trout I had ever eaten (that is for another story, another time).

The carcass looked just like a perfectly cleaned rat, maybe even smaller. I was worried it would be a small taste, not a filling meal. Again, Jim would prove me wrong.

He placed our squirrel in heavily salted water with red and black pepper flakes to boil over the roaring fire. Once our soup came to a rolling boil, he covered it with a makeshift

Squirrel soup simmering in a metal pot.

you could pull the delicate meat from the bones. It was a fantastic soup. We shared the front and back legs, then put the bones with little meat back in the pot for another boil, which would be our breakfast in the morning.

Before we turned in for bed, we topped off the pot of fine broth with more heavily salted water and secured the tin foil cover. The meat and bones melted away during the long morning simmer. The organs were devoured at dinner while the marrow and meat thickened the morning's meal.

That is how I learned to snare squirrels, and so much more.

Red Squirrel organ meats in metal cup, ready for cooking.

Red Squirrel dressed and ready for cooking.

Made in the USA
Middletown, DE
15 October 2023